HENCEFORCE

also by Kamden Ishmael Hilliard

distress tolerance, 2016 (Magic Helicopter Press)
Perceived Distance from Impact, 2017 (Black Lawrence Press)

HENCEFORCE
A TRAVEL POETIC

KAMDEN ISHMAEL HILLIARD

OMNIDAWN PUBLISHING
OAKLAND, CALIFORNIA
2019

Cover and interior text set in Coriander Std, Avenir LT Std, and Joanna MT Std

Cover and interior design by Gillian Olivia Blythe Hamel

Printed in the United States
by Books International, Dulles, Virginia
On 55# Glatfelter B19 Antique
Acid Free Archival Quality Recycled Paper

Library of Congress Cataloging-in-Publication Data

Names: Hilliard, Kamden Ishmael, author.
Title: Henceforce : a travel poetic / Kamden Ishmael Hilliard.
Description: Oakland, California : Omnidawn Publishing, 2018.
Identifiers: LCCN 2018040198 | ISBN 9781632430687 (pbk. : alk. paper)
Classification: LCC PS3608.I4416 A6 2018 | DDC 811/.6--dc23
LC record available at https://lccn.loc.gov/2018040198

Published by Omnidawn Publishing, Oakland, California
www.omnidawn.com   (510) 237-5472   (800) 792-4957
10 9 8 7 6 5 4 3 2 1
ISBN: 978-1-63243-068-7

TABLE OF CONTENTS

"we are driving to the interior"

"*Arrival at Santos*," Elizabeth Bishop

SELF PORTRAIT @CURRENT LOCATION

Are yu willing 2 assist w an emergency? Tether superparticle
a la pronoun in a whole nu crew of questions   I call this
1 the precondition of extancy
                                                I bring revelation
2 pragmatism's soft slot   I   2   hav a soft slot bc the bend
seem'd like a condemnation   Specially
wen i   [[onboard in formal pre-flite suotwat]]
elluminate mi soft serve   My soloptic, variable   agency

See how i mean specificity? In is a preposition
noun adverb & adjective
That's gotta stand 4 standin
I assist yr emergency
gash bait   1nce,   after
                              i thot it was
                                   over over over

Lyk, i moved the ball So I hav 2 move
it again? I've been up!   O guess what
                              it rhymes w again

DROPOFF W FAVOR & ADDICTION

No tears No tips No meters No nips [well
mayb] No Lyft No Uber No 1-8
hundo But he wanna kno How yu been?
            Where'd yu go   & why? [whudda guy   won't in

-ter desire] So tho "[y'all] didn't start
the fire" He galk ya down Ugh a drink
-hir Satisfied?   Now asks of MomDad &
            late nite desires   Till so close yu go

Southwest Delta American Air lines
Any   Here   isgud   Fine: the metallic,
edging departures of queer luv-kin Shipped?
            Sure, yu guess Yu need 2 move on But fucc!

What danger cost too much, Patron saintof
Patrón? Skychaplin, dis politic ain't
got a pot dealer 2 piss in   Yu-Me?
Peppery as an amphetamine Pee-

pull'd as a population restriction
Shirtless i'm serviced; shoeless i'm nervous
I'm saying in everyway I've been
            seen @ all   the desks, submitted   Sordid

TRANSIT [HONG KONG–HONOLULU]

I 1stly flirt bc my visa sags: unperks overcooks Fit
2 dye me under a law which i can only subsume
means i 2 would sag: unperk overcook Cluck & kit
Knuck & buck'd body[ody-ody-ody in death Debloom

-ery I dole A doc's note & it'd've been fine but 4 a dude
A mens en boothful unclockability w my 1-nite-only-*oops*
Nationstates luv men bc mens luv the maybe brood of a nuke
I hav no Canto nor Mandarin but kno what 4 who supes

up all salves of the nationstate There are rules here Shiny
International law here 4 queer bureaucratic besting
Lookit this TSA-approved-pre-text 4 smash hiney!
Happi how homeland Securitas reward the gay nesting

instinct The returning more normal: more manner'd Kept
quiet as I've been waged against; Warned about; Wept

SELF PORTRAIT @THE HONOLULU INTERNATIONAL AIRPORT

1.

The bomb is gonna drop so how will we kno
wat 2 call 'anxiety'   wen   we unbody ; un
man the mirror'd sky's tolerance of our microclimatic doom?

A sustained lackadaisical threat: death [& even inside, upon unravelling
about the island, the subject still carries   its qualities
                    Threat] So lyk totally pardon
any thing i've done   that doesn't seem 2 ask what
2 the slave is trade but expansion? Pain? The well tailored
industries of Paradise
                    Airborne [on per diem!] 2 flower
                    our own[ed] bays
                    our own[ed] sports
                    our own   parts of entry

Wenever they drop the bomb   we'll b red
orange yello green blu indigo vio
                              lent / 4 the body moves among destruction
                              & of the body's subsets there are sum who
                              will will others gone Will want 4 nothing
                              but pentultimance: the buffer the buff
                         'd stones of subjugation & product

Paper chase unburdened by others

Even en wastoidism: don't seem
like i'm giving up the free marker
but i'm cumming lol
just gotta lessen my liquor
Lemme find the green
big making button for my nigger
nigger nigger

2.

Wenever   they drop the bomb
Whatever   the bomb could b
Whoever   has the bomb & even
eff

they think yu cute   it mean
sumthin'
2 go home   2 b taken by the thot
of it
Gone

3.

Eff bastion
of sadness
Then clots of threat

&
eff threat
[of sadness]

then "Come on! Anytime you want!
Come on! I be ready for you... but I
ain't gonna be easy."

&
eff cum

min' on
then collapse the nite

Eff yu do
hard dark
&   [thro the self from lite]

& then sort the body
by permissive distaste
Yu should stop but
like keep going it's hot
but i'm hurtfulhurting
Please, all my mes
Cum home

Omg yes shantay   yu stay

4.

A place of slave labor is not a slave place Ess a place of slave labor
People are slaves in a place of slave labor But b4 i'm just like here crying again
What lies amid the infanta of the slave is a question of travel: like going Having
a home Making a home How you know you aren't Are you a home? May i b,
2, Legal Guardian Land? And then like transit social mobility or the wet dream
of nobility The slave identity is extant 4 those carriers of a trauma so large G-d
was like   *this cannot pozsibly fit in my car*

@ TSA the woman has the *same last rame!* Lol & i can't even offer shame
Wonder even eff she kno my surname yt as the freedom papes & market's grain
or y i'm cocaine crop'd telescopic at 10am] & i joke about how we wash our
wallets b4 air travel 4 neither 1 would court risk while walkin around in the
skin they live us in
      I quit smoking wen I realized is sugar is the killing crop & tobacco is
the killing crop Large public destruction Nuclear booming small

Temporal changes in constructions of ytliberalism—& their yunger,
smarter sibling ytneoliberalism & they cousir ytglobalism—demand increasing
systemic efficiency TL; DR Smart phone users demand smart violence & even
be4 that
      That, referring 2 the archipelago's 1st sugar plantations in the early
1800's but really it's basic It updates & sends itself in2 the legislatively slingy
arms of the The 1890 McKinley Tariff Act

Historians of unconsented labor (the slave, the indentured servant,
the sharecropper) hav shifted focus from machineries of *slave making 2 resistance*
studies
      An abridged list of resistances: work stoppage, abortion, wandering
from the field, opium, fire, work slowdowns, running   away, extended

maternity, deviance

which was almost what i
was meaning: my silent black & black film 4getting thru TSA The whole
flite full of fishy corn aerated red wine   The porcelain pin My inward
retch'd out

  1 totally literal tool of power is mediated agency
  The boi asks how i leave the island so often & i only kno what I've
willed myself against What I am unwilling 2 hav done 2 me any longer

5.

The redeye must b lyk a blojob   4 planes
prefer gud aerodrome Thinin in sumthin
determined 2 b moved thru No1 maintain
constant pleasure Does air even like pressure?
@the end of HNL : JFK a man drove me
2 drink whatever i wanted He was what
ever I wanted but didn't do pleasure I thot
this was Buddhist but dude asked on Mai
Tais *Which rum would be best*, he wundr'd,
allowed, *4 the road*, on which he didn't want
Head Mayb I mean resignation is *no*
4 a non-yt My frighty fite thru
the question of identity What it means 2
how a who yu don't kno or even hav done much 2

1ce i flew & didn't let the men do me in2
a *Yoohoo* Drinkable Clinkable I stood Slept
I was quiet as i was kept I saw a whole thing
about Bayard Rustin amongst bolts & stones
of onyx I fell infinite & legible I cried out
my leakages down the whole multitudinous avenues
It's a living These clattered beads Sweat My
habit is homotropic yet i prey w/in the rules:
hunt for the closest home: Hotel Hostel
Hauxdown Houston Ha'u'ula A hapa boi
who works Hawaiian Air bc he wanna go
sumwhere from where he's going Bc where

he's gone he's going again, lil' dancer He's
made little luv The nite gets him down Every
nite All along

6.

Home-heart
Here -heart is in most danger of gettin' smart
cart'd off   Home   is litefingered
                         practiced
                         blodarted &
down 2 fiberglass the dog
food of war I'm not not not not there
2 make friends I'm here 2 weed
I'm here 2 outdance the bulkhead   Durk holy & awoken
thru the deadass plexiglas of this island feeling ,

no no this island feeling

I just want it to pass on by

I'm tryin' 2 cite loneliness in the face of mounting contrarianism
I am never alone   but have   alone
cum @any semblance of self

I'm telling documented concerns of political materialism
I'm telling yu

I'm so happy 2 b here & here & here & here &

SELF PORTRAIT UNDER BLANKET
ON UNITED FLIGHT UA495

No1'd answer my needful   YES   I am enjoying it   not because I shan't
eff I said next 2 Him / of the dress Yes   b [lemme tell yu sum shet   yas

No doomboi 2000 [worry free Deli   I've torqued   off limit,
very fee]   but a plaintive rest yes   hand-made pleasur   2 make a butch *yes*

Jack'd up in His made mind He all   "The Thong Song" 2 is a sing & I
feisty 4 fucc up my   *ooo tex-mex yes*   let his freedom ringme debt Yes

I've consented 2 publik incandescentcy I watch THE FREE STATE OF JONES
not His   black beans only mess Yes   even tho it's mad off brand I let [yes

I do ownership but couldn't He [@ least] let] Him choose a snack box A whiskey
not *not yet not yet not y!et ye!t ye!s! !!!*   a while after unfoldment   So yessening

I 2 hav deposed my decomposed   I am thinking of Molly Bloom I am yes
desire but the nigga is wet Yes   I—less!—I Yes yes yesyeyesyesyesyesyes

SELF PORTRAIT @THE JACKSON HOLE AIRPORT

Macin' my face in the   MEN'S   mite solv the problem

of open access   Solution?: Doom Peace? Hate the word

I'll still do me   a nargl'd nubilty 2 pour 4   or pliant narrative

2 pull from ditchdom   I mean, basically what it boils down

2: Eff I don't tell yu   I'm a fag, yu won't beat the crap out of me

So what want gud American   violence? Not *my* tax duct

butta dongle   Doohickey 4 glazed dysphoric diaspirations My grief

is MSG free   It on   the adollarable menu It is why i don't facepeel

messy but present 4 the tap dance Ground bone 4 my tonal

concerns   On brand Bandstand /in American   just 2 tip

-tow a homo salaried petition thru the backgore   I'm pilling up

my *say can & used against* & court of aw I'm pulling out of my blooded self

4 national cummembration Public partition of martyrdum: my gender

freakin See me absolve See me bubble See me sour of healing

but still 4 the dream: flite Fruitility Pozsibility

SELF PORTRAIT @LAGUARDIA AIRPORT
W FLIGHT CHANGE

I didn't realize   I thot   I'll sow what i've wrought   We weren't
even I was headed   What time was   What time is
    How far are   Cain't a nigga handle they biz? Am I splitting it   Cum w
me Yu will Yu are paying 4 this, yo Yu taking it 2, ain't chu?   Hold on
    I won't eat   I won't hav a time   I hav water   I dry swallow
Cancellation fee   Where's the head   Don't touch my hair Care[do
yu?]   No— No this Left   G-dDamn I said yr other   No yr other
black friend
    Don't bother [wearing] my black

ODE 2 THE AFFECTIVE

A spin of modern panic sets the day strain / 2jacket The
sadass stone Squalor guild Str8 stoic as my A-line FISA who
Cannot confirm my need 2 dent up a few neural certainties
                  BUT EFF IT DID it wouldn't share
                  The day is a "total top"
                  After, it showers me in Wellbutrin
  praise   Haldol praise
                  Amphetamine Salt daze
of my [now] collective common adder Hiss hiss How now do my brain hurt

I hav the rite paranoia
4 1 attorney b provided
4 me: *What kinna* *wo rd is do ngl e? Why* *d o y u n e e d*
m y I D? W h e r e h a v
t h e y h i d d e n the wires?

I'm fucctional 4ward even eff movement is a matter
of concession 2 treatment: hot dog water   Panko facts

We are legally obligated 2 gift all generic medicines
My most mother-in-law-ly wishes
rainbows in 1 gulp   They beat the gnats The bsides:
hide-a-key coke copping in [this literally
happened] a crab shack bathroom
                         A McDonald's bathroom
But i don't do crab   coke   or McDonald's nymore

or cataracts
of sorrow   or the way sumtimes   w no warning
wind would pull   from me
          my ten thousand hundred   pipings

Unstopped Not even   eff   i do luv
a lil' death in me

EFF YU HAV A CONNECTION OUT OF CHICAGO PLEASE APPROACH THE DESK.

None of us board
Perhaps none
among us paid
2 board   or 2 want 2 board

or enter   movements in search of joy   / Lol jk i'm on the upgrade list
It's just early   yet last nite
Last nite i dreamt unmolested legroom & luked no fantasy in the mouth
                              Could we really want
                    2 kno:w:here we got these ideas?
          As eff rot mite bloom us a place not a property

Variance in placédness is freaky as a freedom pape
All PAX ROMANA & shit Existence & hir dividends
articulated en time: can yu wait?? Can yu step forward
please? Can yu put your hands up? Can yu take off
an hour early from work? No? Then yr latelate late! All on the glass
                              all on my back
                              my backs On my
                              barkings   in2
                              the forest & now
                           the trees & nownow
                              the fates
                        move about the cabin
                  freely as i've fed   myself /line after line

29

Crushed by the queue / we wait to contribute
a bloody fee

SELF PORTRAIT @THE LOS ANGELES
INTERNATIONAL AIRPORT

The Antechamber mouths   kiss&fly   Bak—4 fomo's sake—
                                 &4th from frontierism
                  2 fantasy's   G-d en the Machina

Nothing, lyk,   n e v e r *again* in LA,,

                      The Home of The Church
                      The Home of The Monomimosic

      Lol, i kno
          movement [the throat ; the fly ; the abstinent tithes (those touchless
miles)]
          Movement is so oscillated   so out the sole pro tech tion from pain

Sooooooz i tipsy all intractable like   Luv,even, in this sunglass pleasure
                                    Nutritional beneficence

          But difference wills our escape of the dream Machina
          un2 the dream
All along All a side I always know where I am by the way that the road looks.
Like I just know that I've been here before. I just know that I've been stuck here,
like this one fucking time before, you know that?

1nce they reached
  from their edges in
expansive joy

                    Put it in the small bin No,
                    everything out Is this yours
                    ?Clear Clear Clear?

The emergent Affect Studies mite imagine Ms. Dash fleeing 2 fleeing from fleeing 4
                                                                        or

NO GAME @THE MINNEAPOLIS-ST. PAUL
INTERNATIONAL AIRPORT'S BOOKSTORE

The airport bookstore is an anonymous [there4 sexual] experience
A personal [there4 sexual] experience   They stock Milkweed: anon
-ymous & personal [there4 sexual] fact
     & in an unmediated emancipation of rage that @s @bookstoreboi
     I ask 'em / demand 'em / remand 'em in2 identical erasureality:

   O do y'all hav Ada Limón's new collection?
I actually don't work here.
   O I'm sorry. I justthot—
O, its' cool. I love tht collection, too. Its quiet racialization is faaabulous. It's not even heavy handed.
Like it's not like a 'r a c e b o o k'

       They wanna kno where I go 2 school & upon receipt & review
of materials   I declared enrollment in *The School of Hard Cock*
It was a viscous [there4 sexual] experience: his leaving [sexual
as my maybes] was a loud way 2 loneness   & needed 2 be offer'd

Dead dick Dead dudes Dead gendered deodorant Dead law
                       which could even liken in2
                       dead property [whole filthy
                       shined mean]
         We could thro a dead party! Wonder
                eff there's like   any way 2 kill
      what's killing me   eff it seem   i need the killing

THIS IS THE BARTENDER FROM FREDDY'S
EFF YU DON'T CUM BAK 2 SETTLE YR CHECK
IM CALLING THE COPS

Uh, hi,   Mx.-Race-Merica   Yu hav an account
2 settle Start up that labor shop! Don't shimmy
Don't think less / about yr self in the next want
Unnozzled   Even the ditches would sell
4 the rite   of unmolested assembly! Lookit this stuff
isn't it neat? I got an outbox in lieu of a body,
tapas, pupus, & aperitifs 4 the same purposeful
doing   But yu thot 2 leave   unchecked Luk,
we all talk We all no yu owe dis plastoral nite
a wallet wingéd A wallet emptied A wallet
wide w knowing A wallet w doors & wind
ows A slim fit feeling lyk pig's blood
down the money clit & unfortunately, our payment
programs can't even w yr hard cash   We
don't self-identify as—lyk—super superior   but are
watchful sounds Selfish mostly We dlite   American
as an almanac of Afro-Diasporic aphrodisiacs
These delicacies ain't a decision & disruption of such
articulates yr racial future in memorandum
                    & of yr alleged "nigger wealth"
or naps [even in the nice shit]   it seems yu wish
2 pack it all back in2 a nameless thing   Really nude
color'd 2 nothing in a honest presentism   What eff
we banished the astral bit [the drool the info holder

tool] & really considered how Hundun became Wonton
What eff being named is like the end of possibility?
But O, Kam, yu kno, what 1 won't call themselves 4 what
1 will   scrub themselves nameless   Risk 4 thrill

YA SPEAKER COLLECTS A NU PROBLEMATIC FAVE

Ryan Lochte's eatableass clapp'd
hu, me? I'm hurt, 2   Me hurt, 2 & pissin off
ny imagined community / populish category
Black Twitter 2 #best #beat #break #drag & #bleed
unvetted desire   Fetish

White mens bcum bois in the press statements of white violence

> later regret
>
> > a mistake

#same :!: my national member   shit stir
@themention of Lochte's turquoise / blu enuf 2 bleed / my rock
Tho i   2   hav pissed in foreign streets, hav,   2,
medically induced die-a-betes

> Ooooop lol just me urgent break down door feelin?

I pissed on a Hong Kong department store door
a week in2 summer's ketotic gaze

I / 2   certainly am a bummer   yet
allow luv: yellow cocktail music

SELF PORTRAIT @THE BALTIMORE WASHINGTON INTERNATIONAL AIRPORT

Dun 'em a 10/10   far as this again goes
I'd been hourly in search of reliant blud
Task orient'd   My smile marches wunderin   mayb this 1
                                            pleasing gud 4ever   Beautiful
                                kirk Flood plain

I had em   deliverable / delivered
    left em   disposable / disposed Thicc salt
                            slime amidst
        this dayold cat's eye of mine   Gross I kno   &apparently   people
                            check the acrymonials
                    prepurchase: MLA FBI TSANSA
                    APAFAQ
                        ATMDDFCIA

Who denies logic 4 anything   but pleasure?
Not me ,the name, i call myself   in answer
2 grand transience, ,
            but the well-lit fear
of a terror capable   even in the endtimes

Until then,   the bathroom is about sisters   not twins—kin—cousins!
1 dozen minutes of safe plumbing among which
2 beat! Thanks, temporal drainage Thanks, industrial
time Thanks, threat level The least sorry makeup

early in the 12 hr clock   Wen men no tiene
takes 2 double   nor models or makes of violence

It's the golden hour,   wen yr day old polishes
could b problems   of race Mayb   this luv   that left
made sure yu saw him   [even eff flooded red
plump black]   Mayb it's the lite Who
is coming?   In all fairness   they were soft
wen they begged   They might've said come back

NOTHING ASKS 2 B MADE

Who needs slaves hm? That's fucced, 'Meriqua Sexy jockstrap? Jock jockstrap?

Nah, breh We kno: Earth make a gr8 gourd empty, but we won't Such noble

propensity 4 sum: no, my G-d is cooler shit Henceforce ya grrl's piety is autonomy

Alternatively   cuz i could die any sec don't mean i shouldn't Yu want the truth?

Yu can't handle my damage, Heather It's damage, Heather I snooze lyk a whore

& snore from the jockstrap   [thx, Smackdaddy] Tho mayb my lumps work nothing

but luv Nothing free Nothing impatient [truly] 2 b made off w out w / buyable

but damned w demand for another drink   Another piggy bank clink clinkclink

BLU ORGY

Proximity Nvr the bride's
maid always the booty call Gud
service Bars Hear me, gulping the shore Lap by lap
Post-ethic of decay I relied upon a public
                    but quickly grew
              2 prefer a digital humanities

Digitization saves the body

Population explosion? A post-9/11
concern, yeah? Eff i see sumthin
may i swallow ;) A nigga cain't
rush the cockpit & fears the fraternal order
of the middle seat Could I hav a boi
o' the month club?
Thin as an apparition?

              Betwixt me & the blu sky?
tempered glass
              Betwixt me & his blu eye
Blackened ties

       Events Parents Paternal racisms The relativities of unrestricted mobility

Here's 2 yu, hot air balloon
Here's 2 yu, The Hindenburg

As an advocate 4 the self
ya grrl maintain an emphatic set of tears RE security
My autoimmune flitetmares

sumtimes   prep /eration sumtimes   h8 / eration sumtimes fervent

Prayin not 2 abolish pain   but 2 revel in the unreturned
RSVP   Time conflict 2 avoid the dome
[taking it 2] //   Answer the callboarding boarding   & yu
boardboard   bc yu deserve this   Yu are trusted, traveller Yu hav emptied
yr pockets & submitted   4 identification under theirsky

& bc yu deserve this, it hella hurts less wen nativist-sun-dudebro all
        suh?
        surprised @ya sitting bc this section of the craft
is not abt
        more room 2 werq & relax
but   the front of the cabin

yet

        wen we scoot 2 the window [ass not
crotch,   duh]

        wen they brush w the bill of their snap
back [we
        are compelled 2 flutter]

NOTES & ACKNOWLEDGMENTS

Thank you, Hilliards, always, even if begrudgingly. Thanks, Hannah.

These poems owe a debt to workshops taken at The University of Hawai'i at Manoa under Dr. Craig Santos Perez. Thanks Craig, yr the homie!

Immense gratitude to the editors of *The Bear Review*, *The Collapsar*, *Nat. Brut*, *The Nashville Review*, *Salt Hill*, and *The Shallow Ends* for publishing early versions of these poems.

"DROPOFF W FAVOR & ADDICTION" borrows language from Billy Joel's "We Didn't Start the Fire."

"SELF PORTRAIT @THE LOS ANGELES INTERNATIONAL AIRPORT" borrows language from Gus Van Sant's My Own Private Idaho.

"SELF PORTRAIT @ THE HONOLULU INTERNATIONAL AIRPORT" borrows language from August Wilson's Fences and Clear Conscience's "Island Feeling."

"YA SPEAKER COLLECTS A NU PROBLEMATIC FAVE" is a response to Olympian Ryan Lochte's fabricated police report in Brazil. The italicized language is from an International Olympic Committee statement regarding the story.

"NOTHING ASKS 2 B MADE" borrows language from *Heathers* and *A Few Good Men*.

Kamden Ishmael Hilliard earned a BA in American Studies from The University of Hawai'i at Mānoa. Kam helps with Jellyfish Magazine and Big Lucks while earning an MFA at The Iowa Writers' Workshop.

henceforce: A Travel Poetic
Kamden Ishmael Hilliard

Cover and interior text set in Coriander Std, Avenir LT Std, and Joanna MT Std

Cover and interior design by Gillian Olivia Blythe Hamel

Printed in the United States
by Books International, Dulles, Virginia
On 55# Glatfelter B19 Antique
Acid Free Archival Quality Recycled Paper

Publication of this book was made possible in part by gifts from:
Mary Mackey
Francesca Bell
Katherine & John Gravendyk, in honor of Hillary Gravendyk
The New Place Fund

Omnidawn Publishing
Oakland, California
Staff and Volunteers, 2018–2019

Rusty Morrison & Ken Keegan, senior editors & co-publishers
Gillian Olivia Blythe Hamel, senior poetry editor & editor, OmniVerse
Trisha Peck, managing editor & program director
Cassandra Smith, poetry editor & book designer
Sharon Zetter, poetry editor and book designer
Liza Flum, poetry editor
Avren Keating, poetry editor & fiction editor
Juliana Paslay, fiction editor
Gail Aronson, fiction editor
SD Sumner, copyeditor
Emily Alexander, marketing manager
Lucy Burns, marketing assistant
Anna Morrison, marketing and editorial assistant
Terry A. Taplin, marketing assistant, social media
Caeden Dudley, editorial production assistant
Hiba Mohammadi, marketing assistant